T0068166

THE ESSENTIAL

BOOK OF

KAKURO 2

Dr. Gareth Moore is the author of a wide range of puzzle books for both adults and children. He gained his Ph.D. at Cambridge University in the field of machine intelligence, later using his experience in computer software research and development to produce the first book of Kakuro puzzles published in the UK. He has a wide range of media interests and also runs several websites, including the online Kakuro site www.dokakuro.com.

Other titles by the same author: *The Essential Book of Kakuro*, *The Essential Book of Japanese Puzzles*, *The Book of Hanjie*, *The 10-Minute Brain Workout*, *The Kids' Book of Number Puzzles*, *The Kids' Book of Sudoku: Challenge Edition*, *The Kids' Book of Hanjie*, *The Kids' Book of Kakuro* and the forthcoming *The Book of Hitori* and *The Kids' Book of Hitori*.

THE ESSENTIAL
BOOK OF
KAKURO 2
AND HOW TO SOLVE IT

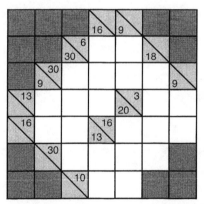

GARETH MOORE

ATRIA BOOKS

NEW YORK   LONDON   TORONTO   SYDNEY

ATRIA BOOKS
1230 Avenue of the Americas
New York, NY 10020

Compilation copyright © 2006 by Michael O'Mara Books Limited
Puzzles and solutions copyright © 2006 by Gareth Moore

Published by arrangement with Michael O'Mara Books Limited

Originally published in Great Britain in 2006 by
Michael O'Mara Books Limited

All rights reserved, including the right to reproduce
this book or portions thereof in any form whatsoever.
For information address Atria Books, 1230 Avenue
of the Americas, New York, NY 10020

ISBN-13: 978-0-7432-9956-5

First Atria Books trade paperback edition August 2006

1   3   5   7   9   10   8   6   4   2

ATRIA BOOKS is a trademark of Simon & Schuster, Inc.

Manufactured in the United States of America

For information about special discounts for bulk purchases,
please contact Simon & Schuster Special Sales at
1-800-456-6798 or business@simonandschuster.com.

HOW TO PLAY KAKURO

Kakuro involves placing the numbers 1 to 9 into a square grid in the same way that letters are placed into a crossword. Unlike a crossword, however, the clues are given *within* the grid. The aim is to make each "run" of horizontal or vertical squares add up to the total printed at the start of that run. You can't, however, repeat a number within the answer to a clue—that is, within a run—in the same way that Su Doku also forbids this. In fact, if you're good at Su Doku then some of the tactics used to complete those puzzles will also help with solving Kakuro.

So that's the theory—now let's look at a typical Kakuro puzzle:

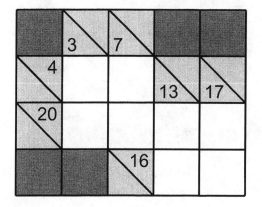

The clue numbers below the diagonal lines give the total of the run of continuous white squares below—so, for example, the "3" means that the two squares below must add up to 3. Similarly, the numbers to the right of the diagonal lines give the total to which the squares to the clue's right must add up—so, for example, the "16" means that the two squares on its right must add up to 16.

All of the puzzles in this book are designed so that you will *never* need to guess, and so that there is only ever *one* solution. For example, the only solution to the above puzzle looks like:

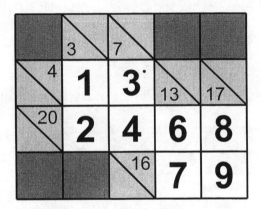

HOW TO SOLVE KAKURO

So how can you get from the empty grid to the finished puzzle above? It's pretty simple really. It's all about remembering that you can only use the numbers 1 to 9, and you cannot ever repeat a number within the solution to any one clue.

Let's look at the top-left white square, where the "3" and "4" clue runs intersect. The solution to the clue "3" must be 1 and 2, because these are the only two numbers in the range 1 to 9 that add up to 3. Similarly, the solution to "4" must be 1 and 3 because these are the only two numbers that add up to 4—we can't use 2 and 2 because this would repeat a number in the same run.

So the top-left square must contain 1 or 2 from the down clue and 1 or 3 from the across clue. It's clear, then, that the only number in common is 1, so we can write this in:

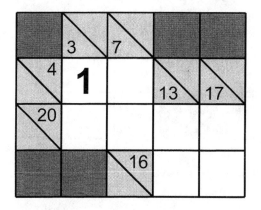

With this square completed, filling in the adjacent two squares is just simple math—and it really is simple, like all the math in Kakuro! In fact, Kakuro isn't really about math at all; with just a little practice you'll remember that the solution to

"4" is always 1 and 3 without having to think about it. To help you you'll find a set of tables at the end of this introduction which list all the possible solutions for every clue and run-length combination, meaning that literally no adding-up need ever be required.

Write in the numbers 3 and 2 next to the 1 in order to satisfy the clues, and then you can also complete the solution to the clue "7" since only one square of it will remain unfilled. The grid now looks like this:

You can also solve the bottom-right square, where the "17" and "16" clue runs intersect, in a similar way. The only two-number solution to the clue "17" is 8 and 9; similarly, the only two-number solution to "16" is 7 and 9. The number in common here is 9, so this must go in the very bottom-right square. Completing the rest of the puzzle is then simplicity itself. You should end up with the completed grid shown previously.

SOLVING TIPS

You can get even speedier results with the following hints:

- Start by looking for clues for which you know only one set of numbers will fit, such as "3" and "4" in the example above, particularly if these intersect with other similar clues.

- Also start by looking at the shortest clue runs. These are often the easiest to solve because typically there are fewer possibilities.

- Lower-value clues are also often easier to solve, simply because the numbers involved are smaller and therefore easier to work with.

- Once you've narrowed down the possibilities for a square, write these in as small numbers with a pencil—then cross them out later as you eliminate them. Not only will this save you from having continually to recheck these clues while you solve others, but it will also give you a visual hint as to where you're most likely to make progress next.

- If the solution to a clue must contain a particular number, such as "3," then don't forget to check to see if there's only one place it will fit in the respective clue run—if so then you can write it in.

- If two squares in a run share the same two possible numbers and contain no other possibilities (or three squares share three possibilities, and so on), then these numbers can't occur anywhere else in the run. If they did then there'd be no solution to at least one of the two squares!

- When, as in the previous tip, you have two squares sharing only two numbers (or three squares sharing three, and so on), then the rest of the squares in that run must add up to the clue total minus the sum of those two numbers.

- Don't forget to use the number-combination tables on the following pages to help you check out the possible clue answers if you can't see what to do next. It will let you find out easily, for example, what the possible solutions to 22 in a 3-square run are (5, 8, 9 and 6, 7, 9, as it happens).

If you get stuck on a puzzle then just go on to another one—there are lots to choose from. Alternatively, you could check the solutions at the back to make sure you haven't gone wrong somewhere along the line (although you'll usually know pretty quickly when you have), and then "steal" an extra number into the grid to help you on your way.

LEVELLING UP

Not all Kakuro puzzles are created equal, so the puzzles in this book are broken down into five distinct levels. Levels 1 and 2 are all small puzzles that are fast to complete, with level 2 being just slightly more challenging than level 1. These puzzles typically take anything from around thirty seconds to five minutes to complete, although if you're new to Kakuro they may take longer at first.

Levels 3 and 4 are at the same respective skill levels as levels 1 and 2, but now the puzzles are larger so they'll take you longer to solve. With a bit of practice you should be able to get the completion time down to around five to ten minutes on most of these!

Level 5 cranks up the difficulty a notch with a mix of puzzles at a moderate skill level—you shouldn't find these too hard by the time you've completed the previous eighty puzzles. They are of all sorts of sizes, so just pick out a puzzle of the type you feel like solving.

COMBINATION (UN-)LOCK

These tables are filled with every possible combination of numbers that you could ever need when playing Kakuro. Just find the table that corresponds to the length of the clue you're trying to solve and then look up the value of the clue in the first column—this will then reveal all the possible solutions to that clue.

The top and bottom few rows of each table have the least number of combinations, so these are the clues to look out for first when you're trying to solve a puzzle.

CLUE RUNS OF LENGTH 2:

3: 1,2
4: 1,3
5: 1,4; 2,3
6: 1,5; 2,4
7: 1,6; 2,5; 3,4
8: 1,7; 2,6; 3,5
9: 1,8; 2,7; 3,6; 4,5
10: 1,9; 2,8; 3,7; 4,6
11: 2,9; 3,8; 4,7; 5,6
12: 3,9; 4,8; 5,7
13: 4,9; 5,8; 6,7
14: 5,9; 6,8
15: 6,9; 7,8
16: 7,9
17: 8,9

CLUE RUNS OF LENGTH 3:

6: 1,2,3
7: 1,2,4
8: 1,2,5; 1,3,4
9: 1,2,6; 1,3,5; 2,3,4
10: 1,2,7; 1,3,6; 1,4,5; 2,3,5
11: 1,2,8; 1,3,7; 1,4,6; 2,3,6; 2,4,5
12: 1,2,9; 1,3,8; 1,4,7; 1,5,6; 2,3,7; 2,4,6; 3,4,5
13: 1,3,9; 1,4,8; 1,5,7; 2,3,8; 2,4,7; 2,5,6; 3,4,6
14: 1,4,9; 1,5,8; 1,6,7; 2,3,9; 2,4,8; 2,5,7; 3,4,7; 3,5,6
15: 1,5,9; 1,6,8; 2,4,9; 2,5,8; 2,6,7; 3,4,8; 3,5,7; 4,5,6
16: 1,6,9; 1,7,8; 2,5,9; 2,6,8; 3,4,9; 3,5,8; 3,6,7; 4,5,7
17: 1,7,9; 2,6,9; 2,7,8; 3,5,9; 3,6,8; 4,5,8; 4,6,7
18: 1,8,9; 2,7,9; 3,6,9; 3,7,8; 4,5,9; 4,6,8; 5,6,7
19: 2,8,9; 3,7,9; 4,6,9; 4,7,8; 5,6,8
20: 3,8,9; 4,7,9; 5,6,9; 5,7,8
21: 4,8,9; 5,7,9; 6,7,8
22: 5,8,9; 6,7,9
23: 6,8,9
24: 7,8,9

CLUE RUNS OF LENGTH 4:

10: 1,2,3,4

11: 1,2,3,5

12: 1,2,3,6; 1,2,4,5

13: 1,2,3,7; 1,2,4,6; 1,3,4,5

14: 1,2,3,8; 1,2,4,7; 1,2,5,6; 1,3,4,6; 2,3,4,5

15: 1,2,3,9; 1,2,4,8; 1,2,5,7; 1,3,4,7; 1,3,5,6; 2,3,4,6

16: 1,2,4,9; 1,2,5,8; 1,2,6,7; 1,3,4,8; 1,3,5,7; 1,4,5,6; 2,3,4,7; 2,3,5,6

17: 1,2,5,9; 1,2,6,8; 1,3,4,9; 1,3,5,8; 1,3,6,7; 1,4,5,7; 2,3,4,8; 2,3,5,7; 2,4,5,6

18: 1,2,6,9; 1,2,7,8; 1,3,5,9; 1,3,6,8; 1,4,5,8; 1,4,6,7; 2,3,4,9; 2,3,5,8; 2,3,6,7; 2,4,5,7; 3,4,5,6

19: 1,2,7,9; 1,3,6,9; 1,3,7,8; 1,4,5,9; 1,4,6,8; 1,5,6,7; 2,3,5,9; 2,3,6,8; 2,4,5,8; 2,4,6,7; 3,4,5,7

20: 1,2,8,9; 1,3,7,9; 1,4,6,9; 1,4,7,8; 1,5,6,8; 2,3,6,9; 2,3,7,8; 2,4,5,9; 2,4,6,8; 2,5,6,7; 3,4,5,8; 3,4,6,7

21: 1,3,8,9; 1,4,7,9; 1,5,6,9; 1,5,7,8; 2,3,7,9; 2,4,6,9; 2,4,7,8; 2,5,6,8; 3,4,5,9; 3,4,6,8; 3,5,6,7

22: 1,4,8,9; 1,5,7,9; 1,6,7,8; 2,3,8,9; 2,4,7,9; 2,5,6,9; 2,5,7,8; 3,4,6,9; 3,4,7,8; 3,5,6,8; 4,5,6,7

23: 1,5,8,9; 1,6,7,9; 2,4,8,9; 2,5,7,9; 2,6,7,8; 3,4,7,9; 3,5,6,9; 3,5,7,8; 4,5,6,8

24: 1,6,8,9; 2,5,8,9; 2,6,7,9; 3,4,8,9; 3,5,7,9; 3,6,7,8; 4,5,6,9; 4,5,7,8

25: 1,7,8,9; 2,6,8,9; 3,5,8,9; 3,6,7,9; 4,5,7,9; 4,6,7,8

26: 2,7,8,9; 3,6,8,9; 4,5,8,9; 4,6,7,9; 5,6,7,8

27: 3,7,8,9; 4,6,8,9; 4,6,7,9; 5,6,7,8

28: 4,7,8,9; 5,6,8,9

29: 5,7,8,9

30: 6,7,8,9

CLUE RUNS OF LENGTH 5:

15: 1,2,3,4,5
16: 1,2,3,4,6
17: 1,2,3,4,7; 1,2,3,5,6
18: 1,2,3,4,8; 1,2,3,5,7; 1,2,4,5,6
19: 1,2,3,4,9; 1,2,3,5,8; 1,2,3,6,7; 1,2,4,5,7; 1,3,4,5,6
20: 1,2,3,5,9; 1,2,3,6,8; 1,2,4,5,8; 1,2,4,6,7; 1,3,4,5,7; 2,3,4,5,6
21: 1,2,3,6,9; 1,2,3,7,8; 1,2,4,5,9; 1,2,4,6,8; 1,2,5,6,7; 1,3,4,5,8; 1,3,4,6,7; 2,3,4,5,7
22: 1,2,3,7,9; 1,2,4,6,9; 1,2,4,7,8; 1,2,5,6,8; 1,3,4,5,9; 1,3,4,6,8; 1,3,5,6,7; 2,3,4,5,8; 2,3,4,6,7
23: 1,2,3,8,9; 1,2,4,7,9; 1,2,5,6,9; 1,2,5,7,8; 1,3,4,6,9; 1,3,4,7,8; 1,3,5,6,8; 1,4,5,6,7; 2,3,4,5,9; 2,3,4,6,8; 2,3,5,6,7
24: 1,2,4,8,9; 1,2,5,7,9; 1,2,6,7,8; 1,3,4,7,9; 1,3,5,6,9; 1,3,5,7,8; 1,4,5,6,8; 2,3,4,6,9; 2,3,4,7,8; 2,3,5,6,8; 2,4,5,6,7
25: 1,2,5,8,9; 1,2,6,7,9; 1,3,4,8,9; 1,3,5,7,9; 1,3,6,7,8; 1,4,5,6,9; 1,4,5,7,8; 2,3,4,7,9; 2,3,5,6,9; 2,3,5,7,8; 2,4,5,6,8; 3,4,5,6,7
26: 1,2,6,8,9; 1,3,5,8,9; 1,3,6,7,9; 1,4,5,7,9; 1,4,6,7,8; 2,3,4,8,9; 2,3,5,7,9; 2,3,6,7,8; 2,4,5,6,9; 2,4,5,7,8; 3,4,5,6,8
27: 1,2,7,8,9; 1,3,6,8,9; 1,4,5,8,9; 1,4,6,7,9; 1,5,6,7,8; 2,3,5,8,9; 2,3,6,7,9; 2,4,5,7,9; 2,4,6,7,8; 3,4,5,6,9; 3,4,5,7,8
28: 1,3,7,8,9; 1,4,6,8,9; 1,5,6,7,9; 2,3,6,8,9; 2,4,5,8,9; 2,4,6,7,9; 2,5,6,7,8; 3,4,5,7,9; 3,4,6,7,8; 3,4,5,6,8
29: 1,4,7,8,9; 1,5,6,8,9; 2,3,7,8,9; 2,4,6,8,9; 2,5,6,7,9; 3,4,5,8,9; 3,4,6,7,9; 3,5,6,7,8; 4,5,6,7,9; 3,4,5,7,9
30: 1,5,7,8,9; 2,4,7,8,9; 2,5,6,8,9; 3,4,6,8,9; 3,5,6,7,9; 4,5,6,7,8
31: 1,6,7,8,9; 2,5,7,8,9; 3,4,7,8,9; 3,5,6,8,9; 4,5,6,7,9
32: 2,6,7,8,9; 3,5,7,8,9; 4,5,6,8,9;
33: 3,6,7,8,9; 4,5,7,8,9
34: 4,6,7,8,9
35: 5,6,7,8,9

CLUE RUNS OF LENGTH 6:

21: 1,2,3,4,5,6
22: 1,2,3,4,5,7
23: 1,2,3,4,5,8; 1,2,3,4,6,7
24: 1,2,3,4,5,9; 1,2,3,4,6,8; 1,2,3,5,6,7
25: 1,2,3,4,6,9; 1,2,3,4,7,8; 1,2,3,5,6,8; 1,2,4,5,6,7
26: 1,2,3,4,7,9; 1,2,3,5,6,9; 1,2,3,5,7,8; 1,2,4,5,6,8; 1,3,4,5,6,7
27: 1,2,3,4,8,9; 1,2,3,5,7,9; 1,2,3,6,7,8; 1,2,4,5,6,9; 1,2,4,5,7,8; 1,3,4,5,6,8; 2,3,4,5,6,7
28: 1,2,3,5,8,9; 1,2,3,6,7,9; 1,2,4,5,7,9; 1,2,4,6,7,8; 1,3,4,5,6,9; 1,3,4,5,7,8; 2,3,4,5,6,8
29: 1,2,3,6,8,9; 1,2,4,5,8,9; 1,2,4,6,7,9; 1,2,5,6,7,8; 1,3,4,5,7,9; 1,3,4,6,7,8; 2,3,4,5,6,9; 2,3,4,5,7,8
30: 1,2,3,7,8,9; 1,2,4,6,8,9; 1,2,5,6,7,9; 1,3,4,5,8,9; 1,3,4,6,7,9; 1,3,5,6,7,8; 2,3,4,5,7,9; 2,3,4,6,7,8
31: 1,2,4,7,8,9; 1,2,5,6,8,9; 1,3,4,6,8,9; 1,3,5,6,7,9; 1,4,5,6,7,8; 2,3,4,5,8,9; 2,3,4,6,7,9; 2,3,5,6,7,8
32: 1,2,5,7,8,9; 1,3,4,7,8,9; 1,3,5,6,8,9; 1,4,5,6,7,9; 2,3,4,6,8,9; 2,3,5,6,7,9; 2,4,5,6,7,8
33: 1,2,6,7,8,9; 1,3,5,7,8,9; 1,4,5,6,8,9; 2,3,4,7,8,9; 2,3,5,6,8,9; 2,4,5,6,7,9; 3,4,5,6,7,8
34: 1,3,6,7,8,9; 1,4,5,7,8,9; 2,3,5,7,8,9; 2,4,5,6,8,9; 3,4,5,6,7,9
35: 1,4,6,7,8,9; 2,3,6,7,8,9; 2,4,5,7,8,9; 3,4,5,6,8,9
36: 1,5,6,7,8,9; 2,4,6,7,8,9; 3,4,5,7,8,9
37: 2,5,6,7,8,9; 3,4,6,7,8,9
38: 3,5,6,7,8,9
39: 4,5,6,7,8,9

CLUE RUNS OF LENGTH 7:

28: 1,2,3,4,5,6,7
29: 1,2,3,4,5,6,8
30: 1,2,3,4,5,6,9; 1,2,3,4,5,7,8
31: 1,2,3,4,5,7,9; 1,2,3,4,6,7,8
32: 1,2,3,4,5,8,9; 1,2,3,4,6,7,9; 1,2,3,5,6,7,8
33: 1,2,3,4,6,8,9; 1,2,3,5,6,7,9; 1,2,4,5,6,7,8
34: 1,2,3,4,7,8,9; 1,2,3,5,6,8,9; 1,2,4,5,6,7,9; 1,3,4,5,6,7,8
35: 1,2,3,5,7,8,9; 1,2,4,5,6,8,9; 1,3,4,5,6,7,9; 2,3,4,5,6,7,8
36: 1,2,3,6,7,8,9; 1,2,4,5,7,8,9; 1,3,4,5,6,8,9; 2,3,4,5,6,7,9
37: 1,2,4,6,7,8,9; 1,3,4,5,7,8,9; 2,3,4,5,6,8,9
38: 1,2,5,6,7,8,9; 1,3,4,6,7,8,9; 2,3,4,5,7,8,9
39: 1,3,5,6,7,8,9; 2,3,4,6,7,8,9
40: 1,4,5,6,7,8,9; 2,3,5,6,7,8,9
41: 2,4,5,6,7,8,9
42: 3,4,5,6,7,8,9

CLUE RUNS OF LENGTH 8:

36: 1,2,3,4,5,6,7,8
37: 1,2,3,4,5,6,7,9
38: 1,2,3,4,5,6,8,9
39: 1,2,3,4,5,7,8,9
40: 1,2,3,4,6,7,8,9
41: 1,2,3,5,6,7,8,9
42: 1,2,4,5,6,7,8,9
43: 1,3,4,5,6,7,8,9
44: 2,3,4,5,6,7,8,9

Good luck!

LEVEL 1

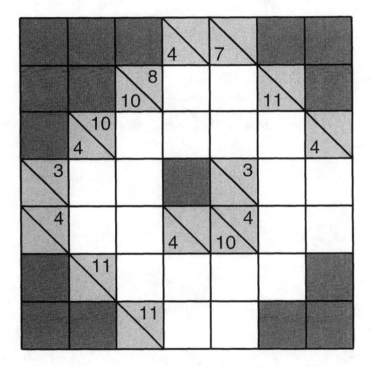

LEVEL 1 • PUZZLE 2

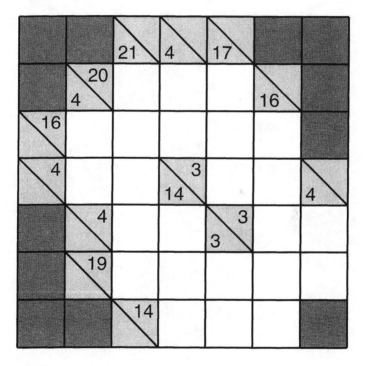

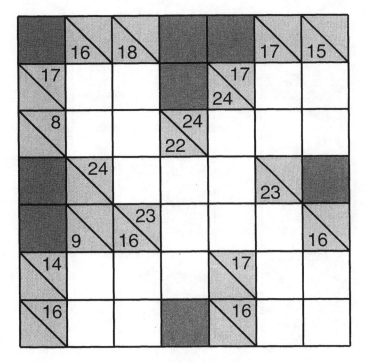

LEVEL 1 • PUZZLE 4

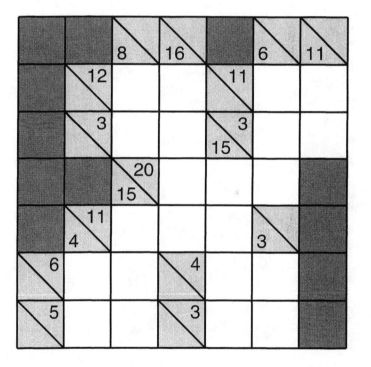

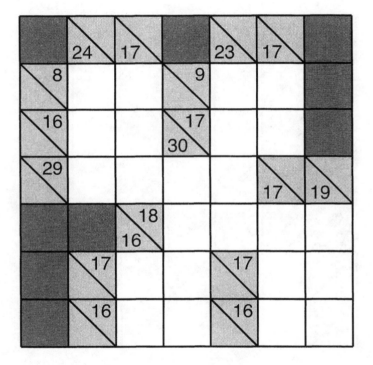

LEVEL 1 • PUZZLE 6

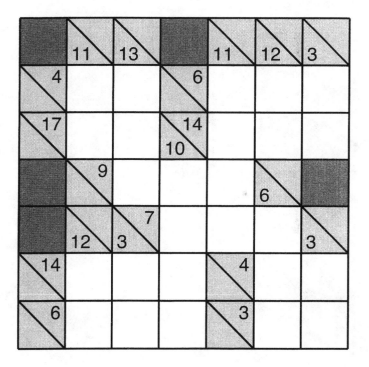

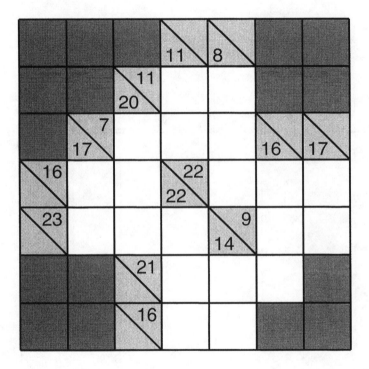

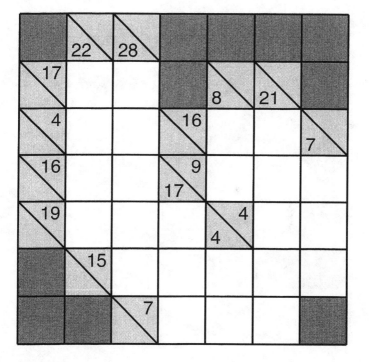

LEVEL 1 • PUZZLE 9

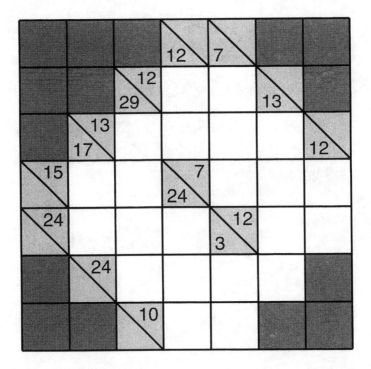

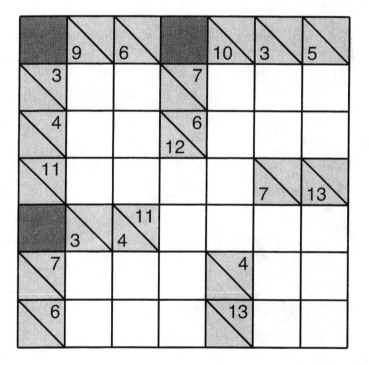

LEVEL 1 • PUZZLE 11

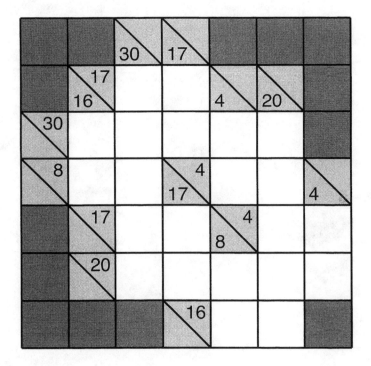

LEVEL 1 • PUZZLE 12

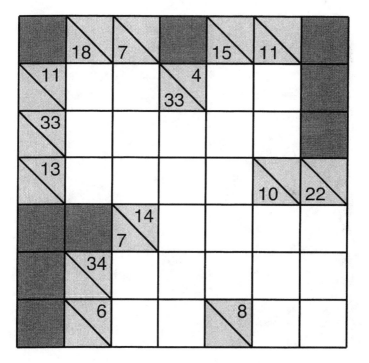

LEVEL 1 • PUZZLE 13

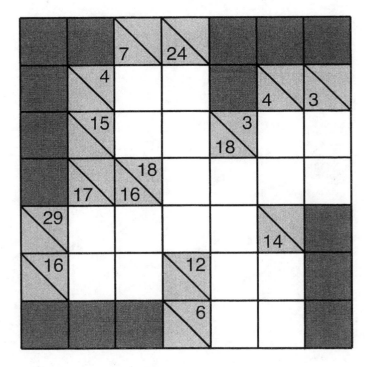

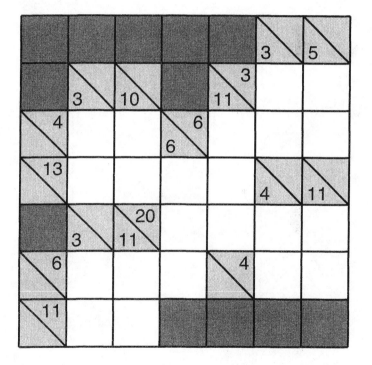

LEVEL 1 • PUZZLE 15

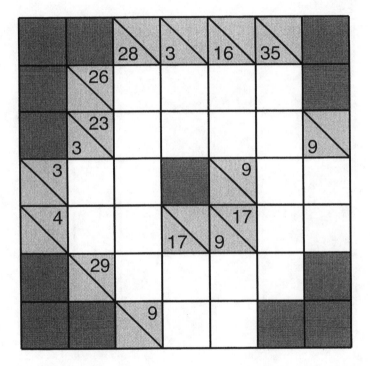

LEVEL 1 • PUZZLE 16

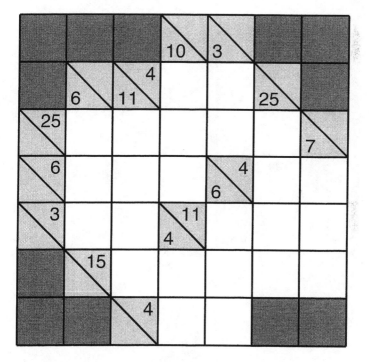

LEVEL 1 • PUZZLE 17

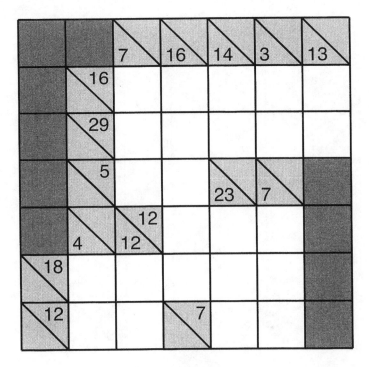

LEVEL 1 • PUZZLE 18

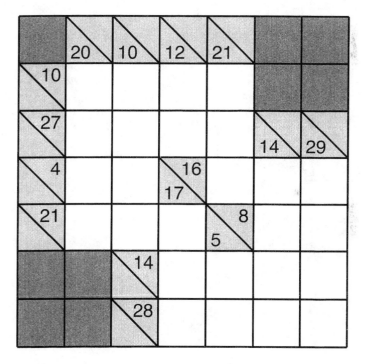

LEVEL 1 • PUZZLE 19

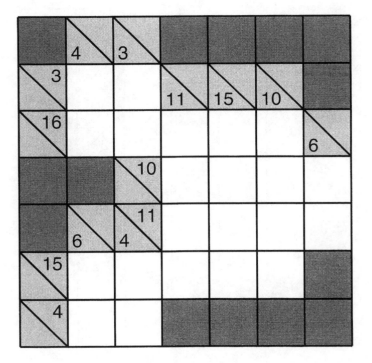

LEVEL 1 • PUZZLE 20

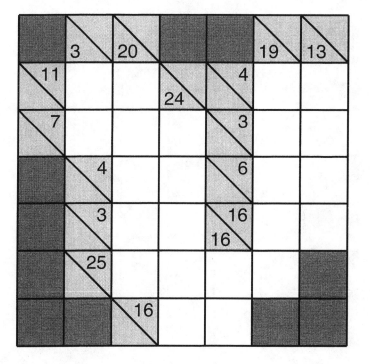

LEVEL 1 • PUZZLE 21

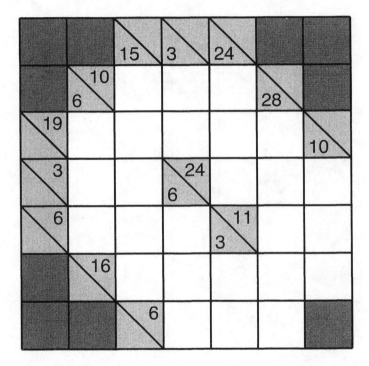

LEVEL 1 • PUZZLE 22

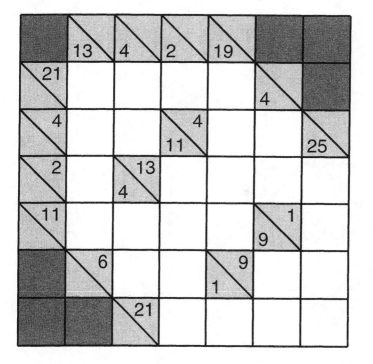

LEVEL 1 • PUZZLE 23

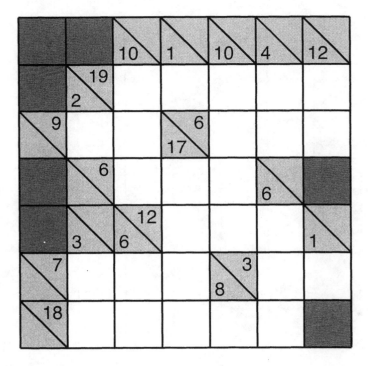

LEVEL 1 • PUZZLE 24

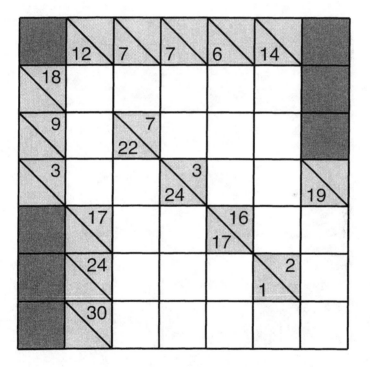

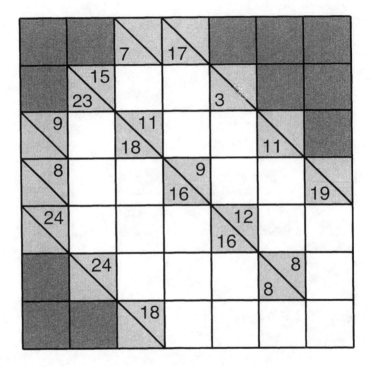

LEVEL 1 • PUZZLE 26

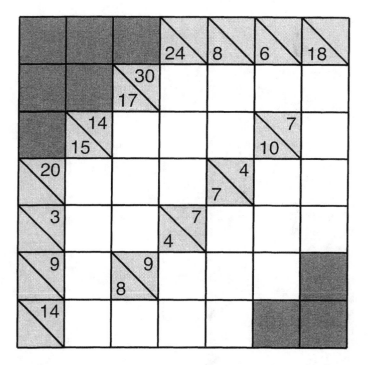

LEVEL 1 • PUZZLE 27

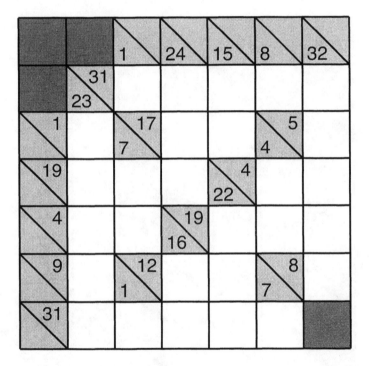

LEVEL 1 • PUZZLE 28

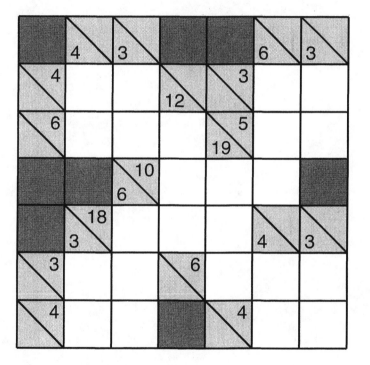

LEVEL 2

LEVEL 2 • PUZZLE 29

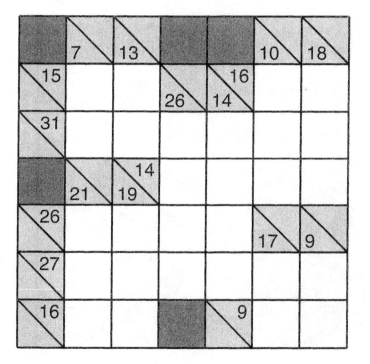

LEVEL 2 • PUZZLE 30

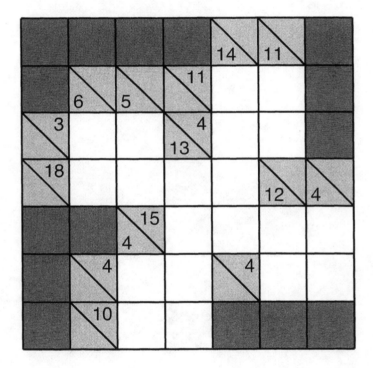

LEVEL 2 • PUZZLE 31

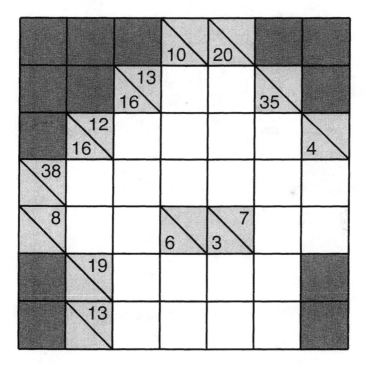

LEVEL 2 • PUZZLE 32

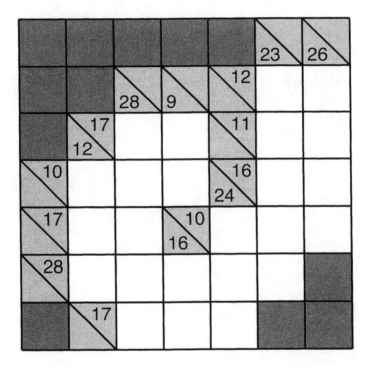

LEVEL 2 • PUZZLE 33

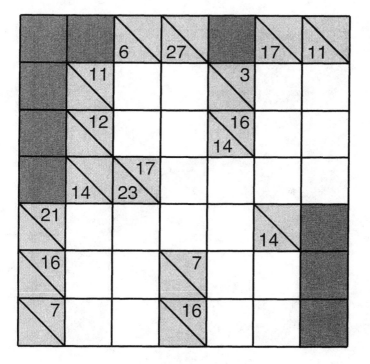

LEVEL 2 • PUZZLE 34

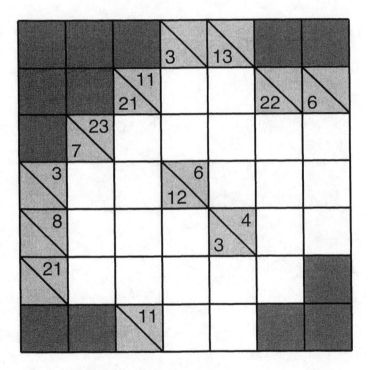

LEVEL 2 • PUZZLE 35

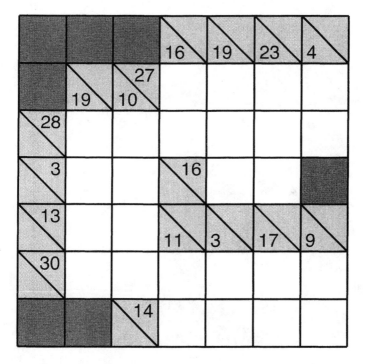

LEVEL 2 • PUZZLE 36

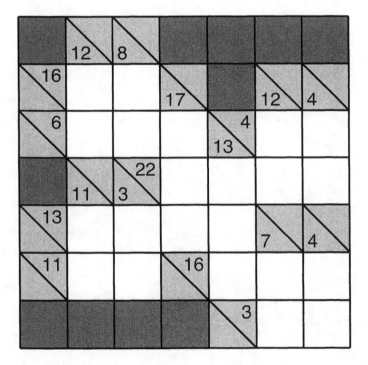

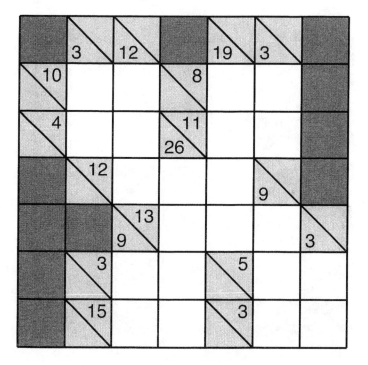

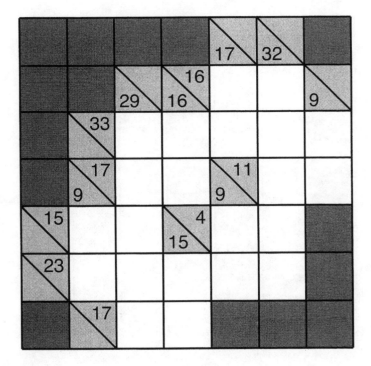

LEVEL 2 • PUZZLE 39

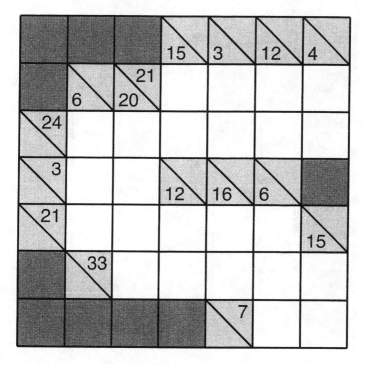

LEVEL 2 • PUZZLE 40

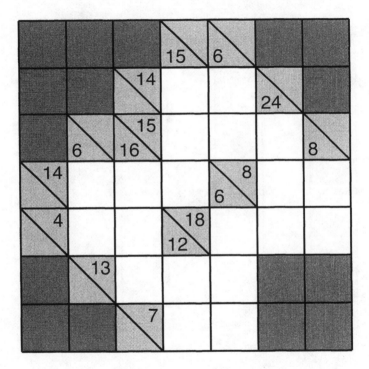

LEVEL 2 • PUZZLE 41

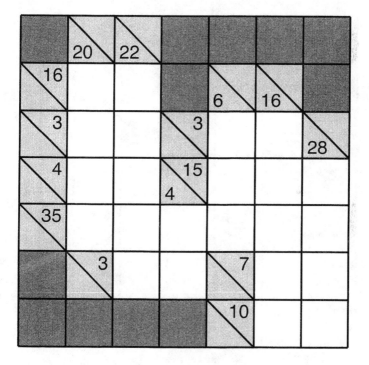

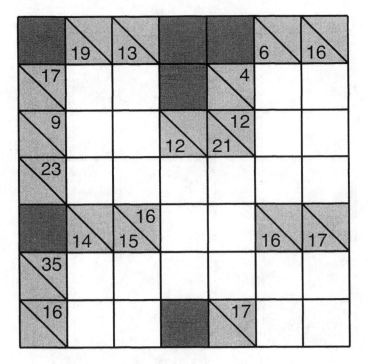

LEVEL 2 • PUZZLE 43

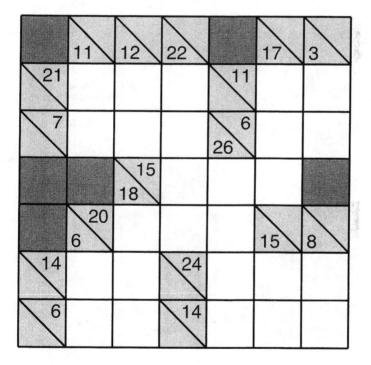

LEVEL 2 • PUZZLE 44

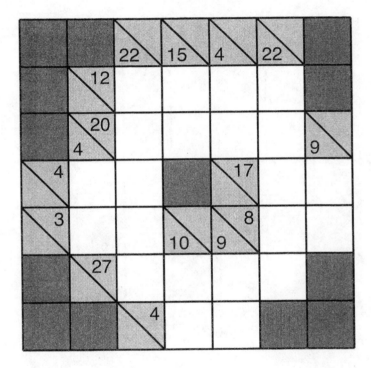

LEVEL 2 • PUZZLE 45

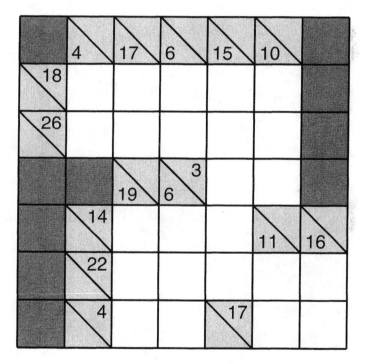

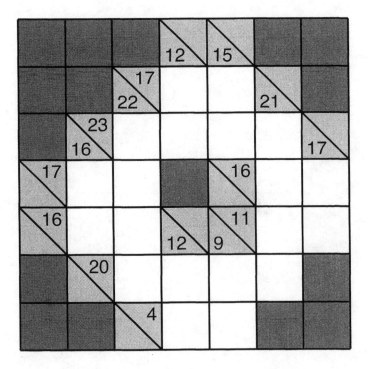

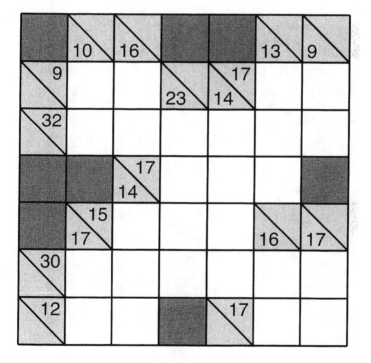

LEVEL 2 • PUZZLE 48

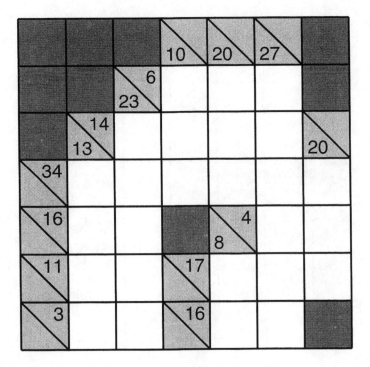

LEVEL 4 • PUZZLE 49

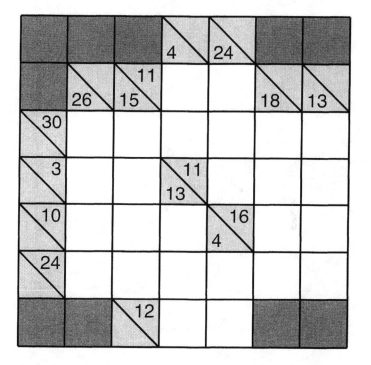

LEVEL 2 • PUZZLE 50

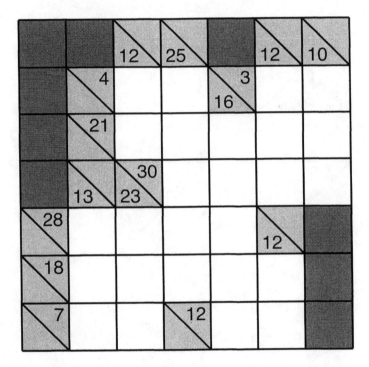

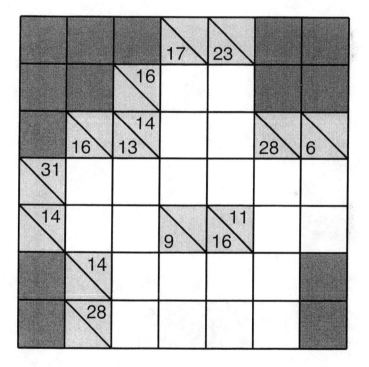

LEVEL 2 • PUZZLE 52

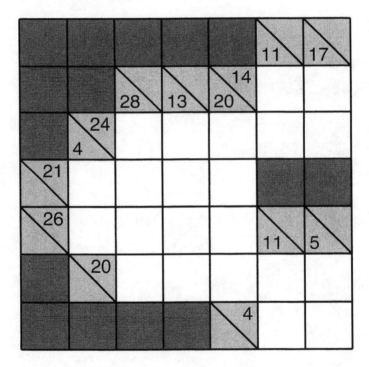

LEVEL 2 • PUZZLE 53

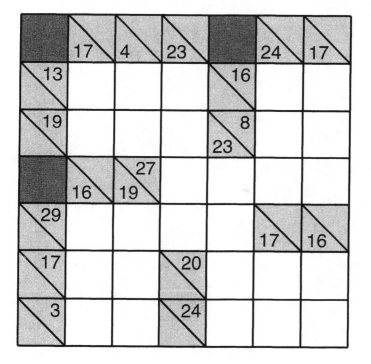

LEVEL 2 • PUZZLE 54

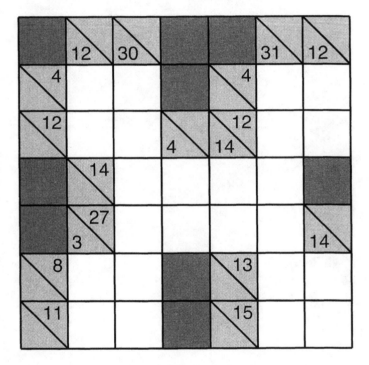

LEVEL 2 • PUZZLE 55

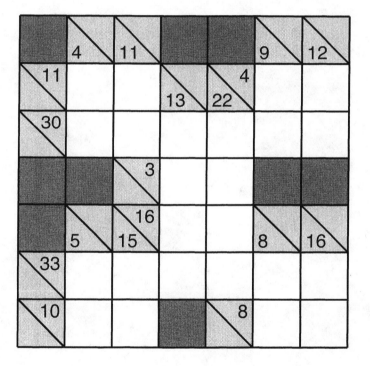

LEVEL 2 • PUZZLE 56

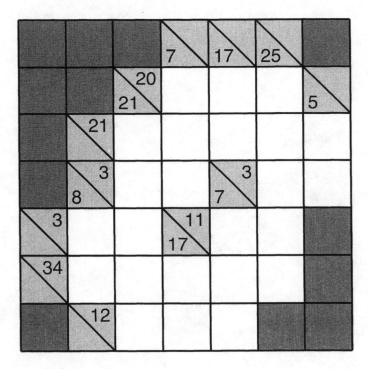

LEVEL 3

LEVEL 3 • PUZZLE 57

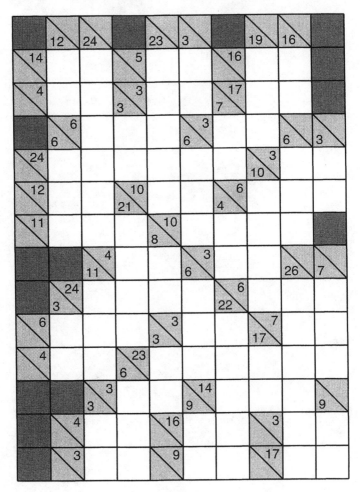

LEVEL 3 • PUZZLE 58

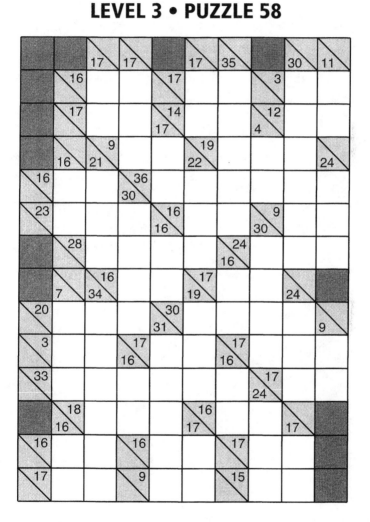

LEVEL 3 • PUZZLE 59

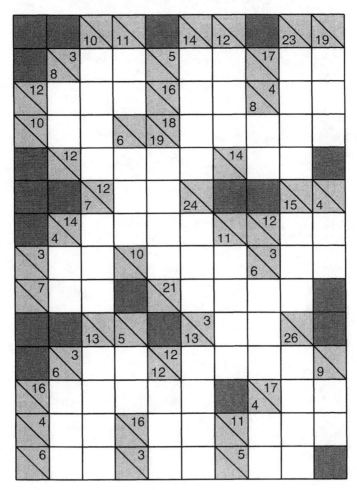

LEVEL 3 • PUZZLE 60

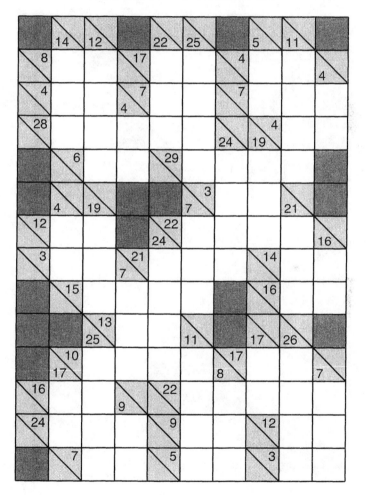

LEVEL 3 • PUZZLE 61

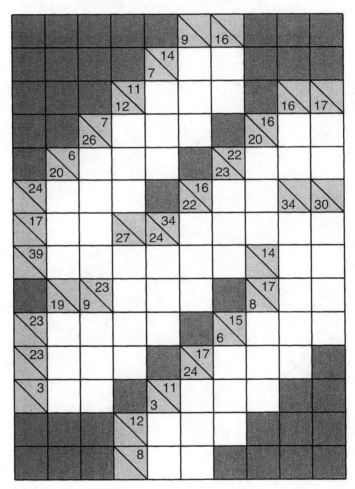

LEVEL 3 • PUZZLE 62

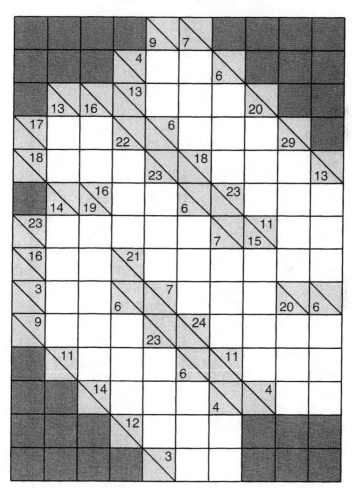

LEVEL 3 • PUZZLE 63

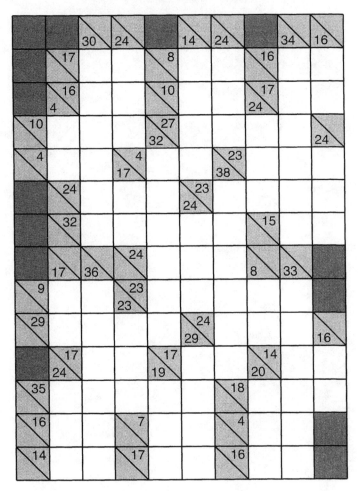

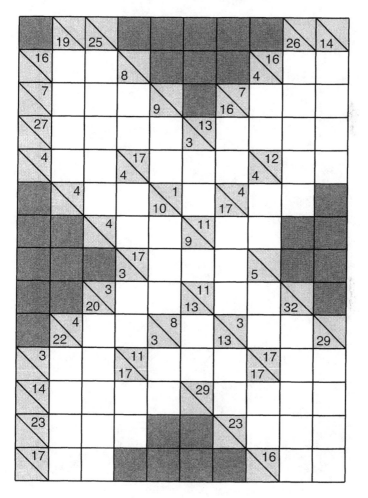

LEVEL 3 • PUZZLE 65

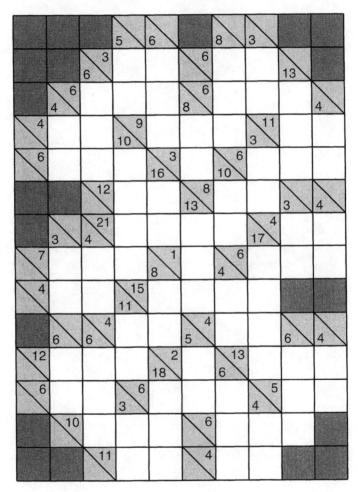

LEVEL 3 • PUZZLE 66

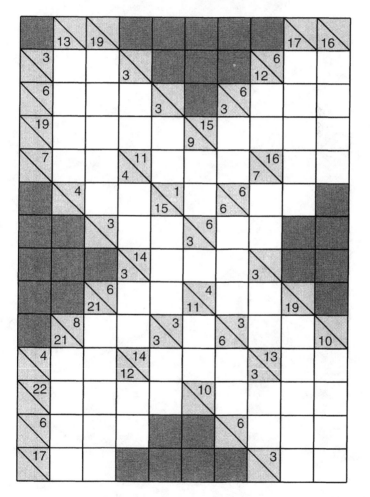

LEVEL 3 • PUZZLE 67

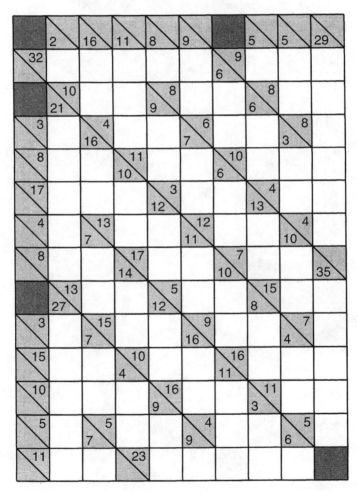

LEVEL 3 • PUZZLE 68

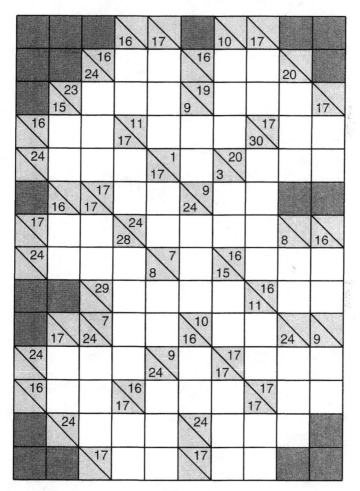

LEVEL 4

LEVEL 4 • PUZZLE 69

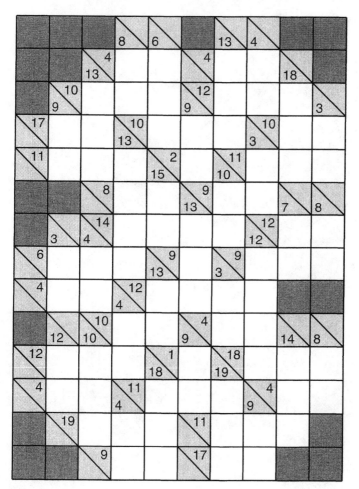

LEVEL 4 • PUZZLE 70

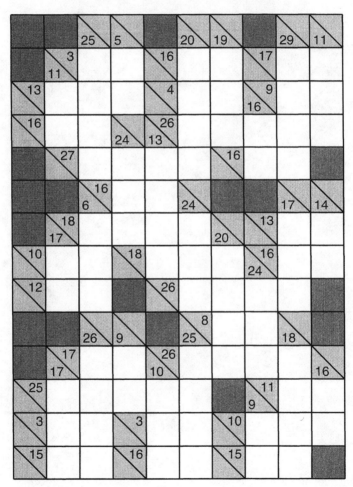

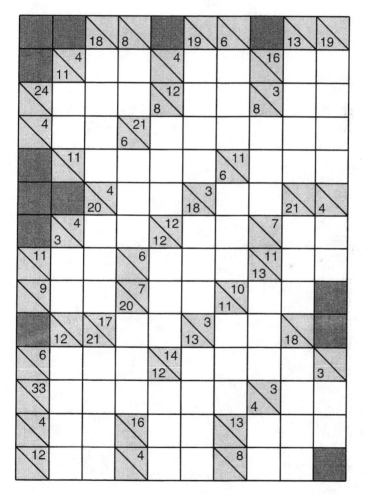

LEVEL 4 • PUZZLE 72

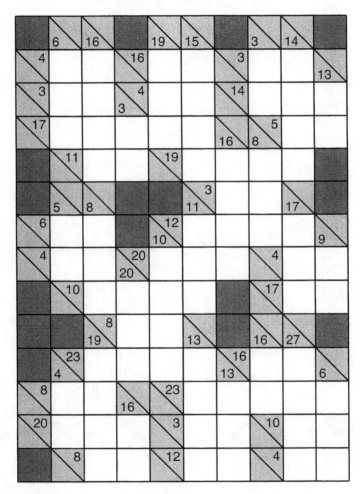

LEVEL 4 • PUZZLE 73

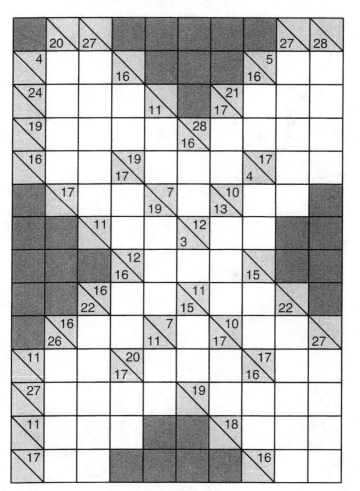

LEVEL 4 • PUZZLE 74

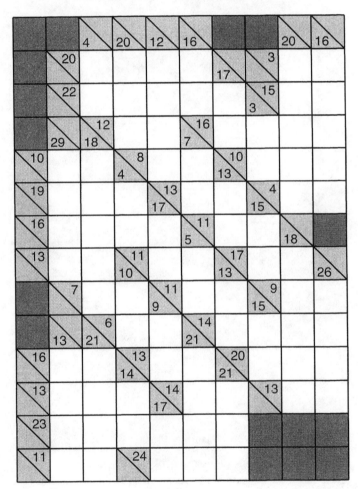

LEVEL 4 • PUZZLE 75

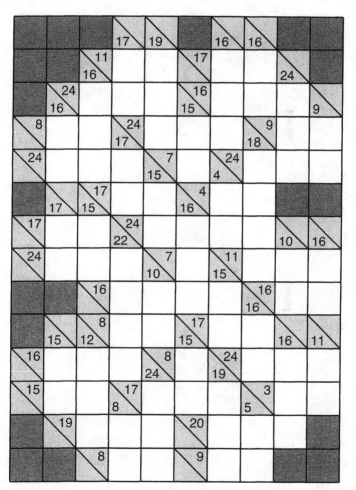

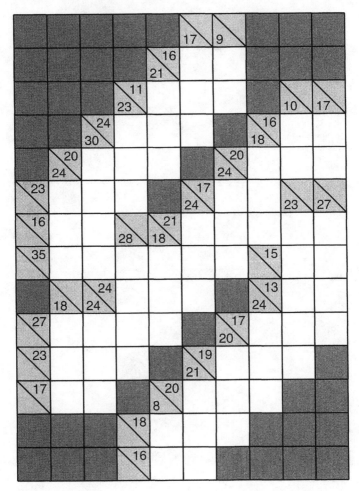

LEVEL 4 • PUZZLE 77

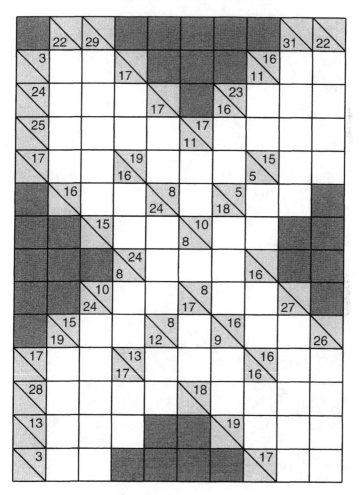

LEVEL 4 • PUZZLE 78

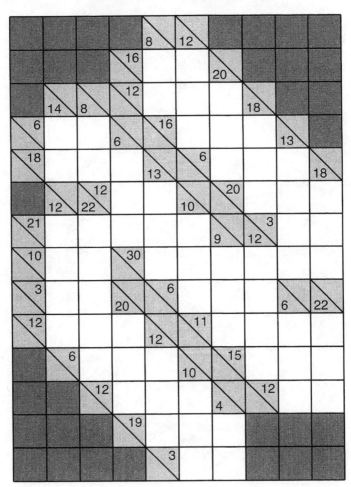

LEVEL 4 • PUZZLE 79

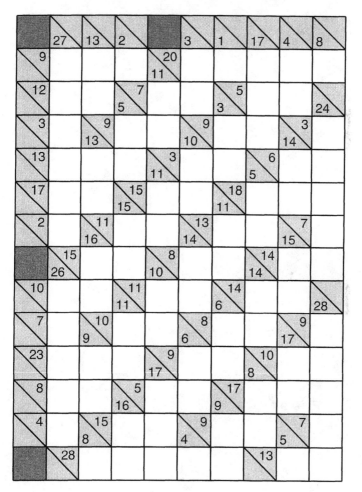

LEVEL 4 • PUZZLE 80

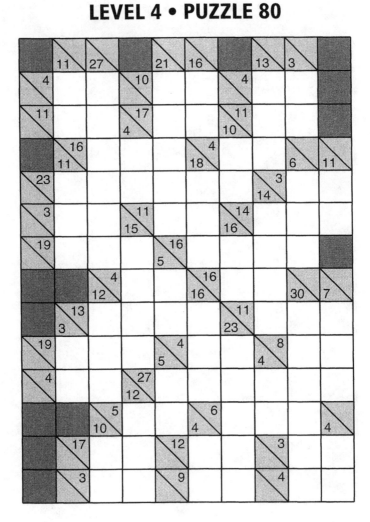

LEVEL 5

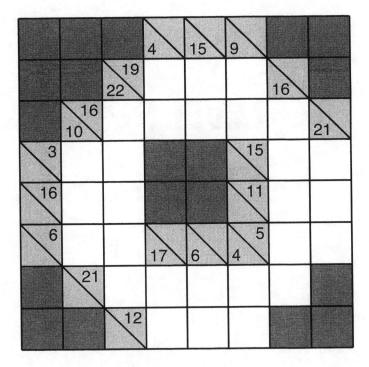

LEVEL 5 • PUZZLE 82

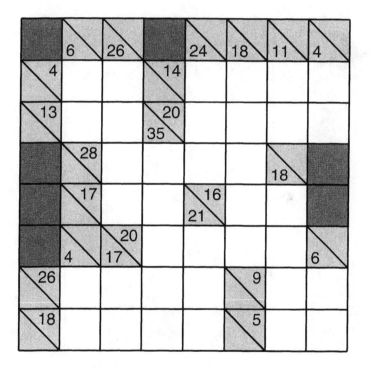

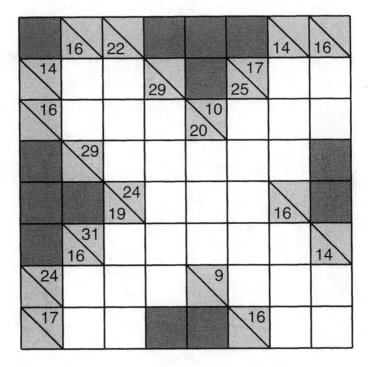

LEVEL 5 • PUZZLE 84

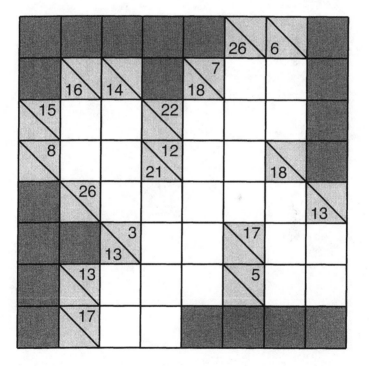

LEVEL 5 • PUZZLE 85

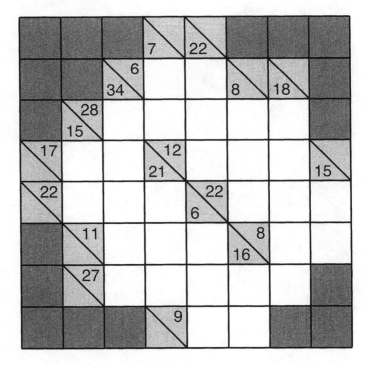

LEVEL 5 • PUZZLE 86

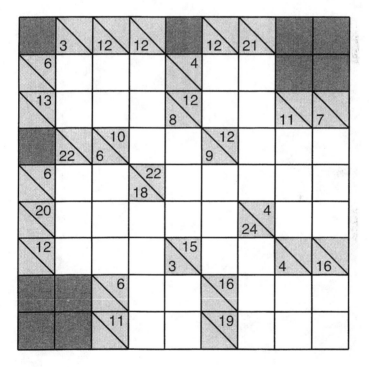

LEVEL 5 • PUZZLE 87

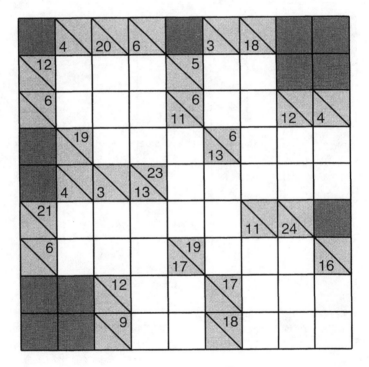

LEVEL 5 • PUZZLE 88

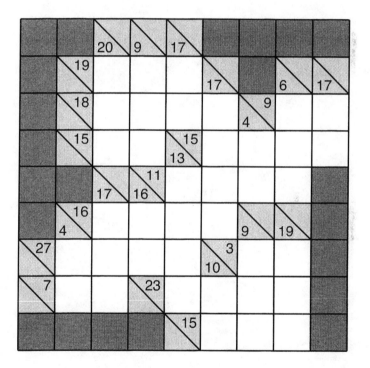

LEVEL 5 • PUZZLE 89

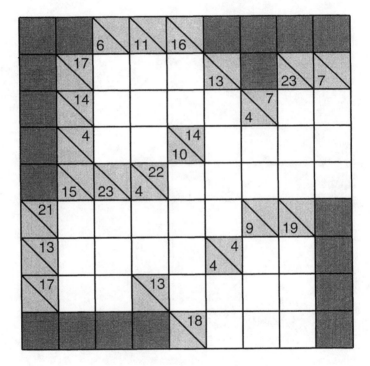

LEVEL 5 • PUZZLE 90

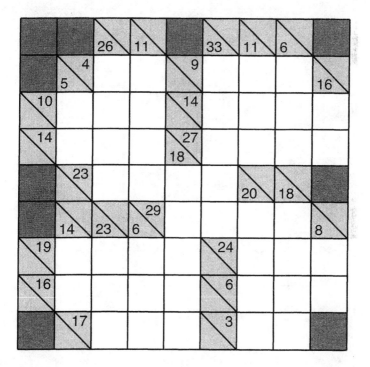

LEVEL 5 • PUZZLE 91

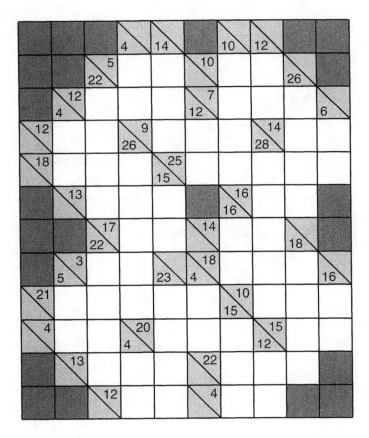

LEVEL 5 • PUZZLE 92

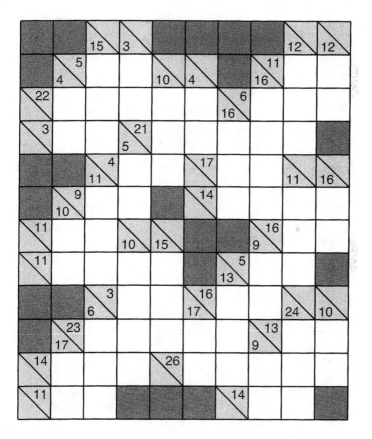

LEVEL 5 • PUZZLE 93

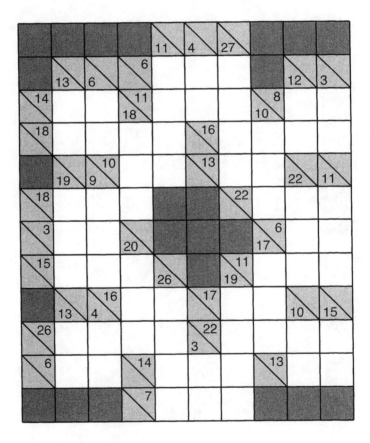

LEVEL 5 • PUZZLE 94

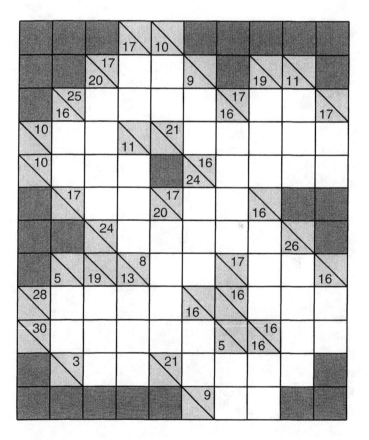

LEVEL 5 • PUZZLE 95

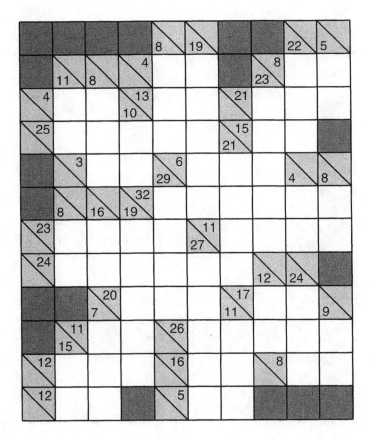

LEVEL 5 • PUZZLE 96

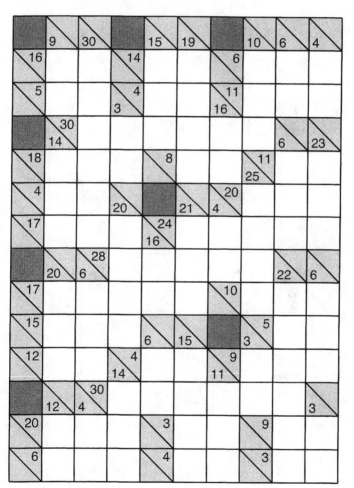

LEVEL 5 • PUZZLE 97

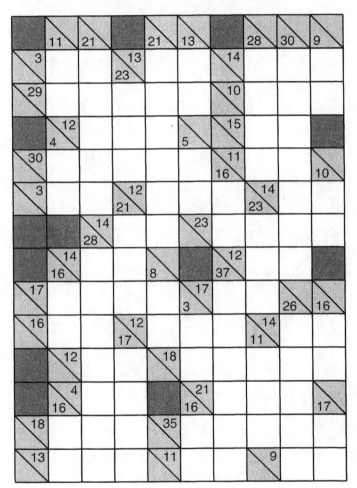

LEVEL 5 • PUZZLE 98

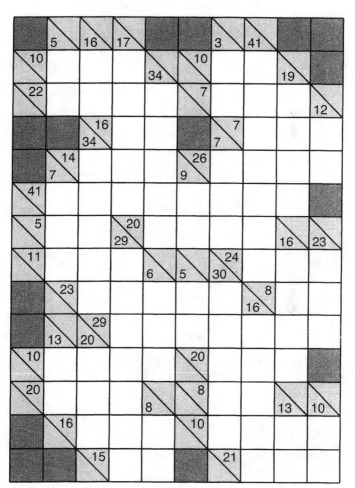

LEVEL 5 • PUZZLE 99

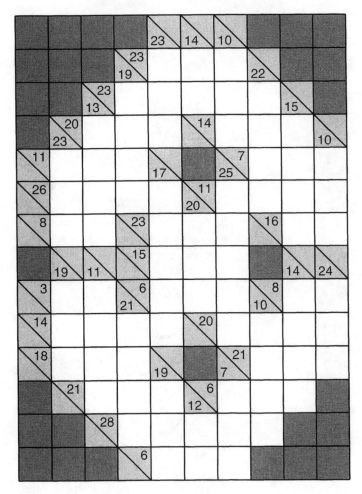

LEVEL 5 • PUZZLE 100

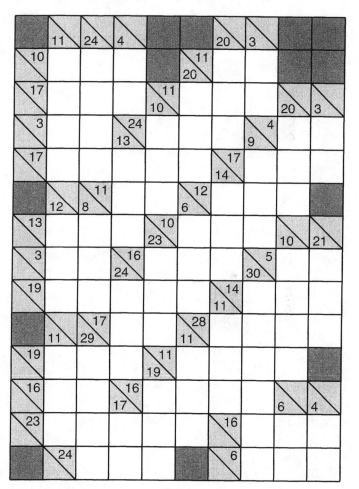

LEVEL 5 • PUZZLE 101

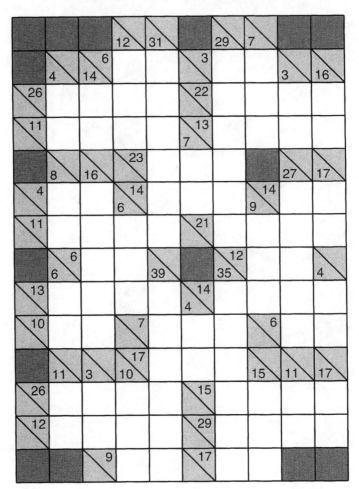

SOLUTIONS

SOLUTIONS

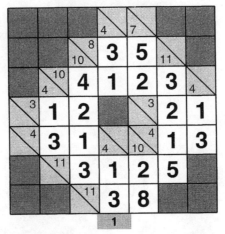

1

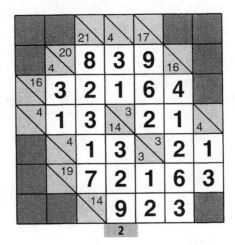

2

SOLUTIONS

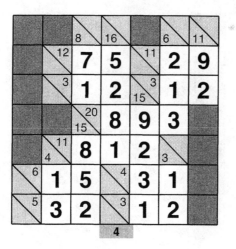

3

4

SOLUTIONS

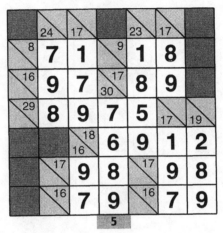

5

	24	17		23	17	
8	7	1	9	1	8	
16	9	7	17/30	8	9	
29	8	9	7	5	17	19
		18/16	6	9	1	2
	17	9	8	17	9	8
	16	7	9	16	7	9

6

	11	13		11	12	3
4	3	1	6	2	3	1
17	8	9	14/10	3	9	2
	9	3	1	5	6	
7	12	3	7	4	1	2	3
14	9	2	3	4	3	1
6	3	1	2	3	1	2

SOLUTIONS

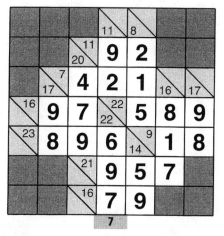

7

8

SOLUTIONS

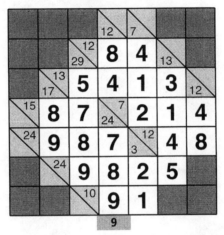

9

			12	7		
		12 29	8	4	13	
	13 17	5	4	1	3	12
15	8	7	7 24	2	1	4
24	9	8	7	12 3	4	8
	24	9	8	2	5	
		10	9	1		

10

	9	6		10	3	5
3	1	2	7	4	1	2
4	3	1	6 12	1	2	3
11	5	3	1	2	7	13
	3	11 4	5	3	2	1
7	2	1	4	4	1	3
6	1	3	2	13	4	9

SOLUTIONS

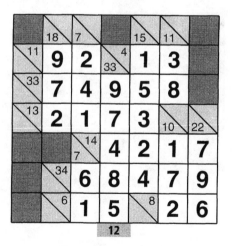

11

12

SOLUTIONS

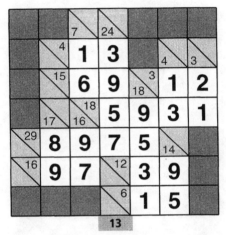

13

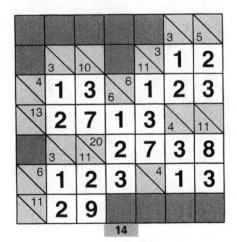

14

SOLUTIONS

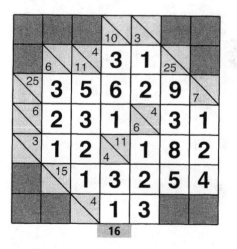

15

16

SOLUTIONS

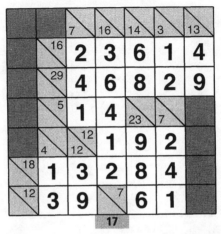

17

18

SOLUTIONS

Puzzle 19

Clues and solution grid:

Across/down clues: 4, 3, 3, 16, 11, 15, 10, 6, 10, 11, 6, 4, 15, 4

	4	3			
3	1	2	11	15	10
16	3	1	2	6	4	6
		10	1	2	3	4
	6	4 / 11	5	3	1	2
15	5	1	3	4	2
4	1	3			

19

Puzzle 20

Clues: 3, 20, 19, 13, 11, 24, 4, 7, 3, 4, 6, 3, 16, 16, 25, 16

	3	20			19	13
11	2	9	24	4	1	3
7	1	2	4	3	2	1
	4	3	1	6	4	2
	3	1	2	16 / 16	9	7
	25	5	8	9	3	
		16	9	7		

20

SOLUTIONS

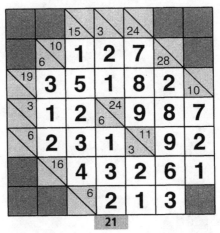

21

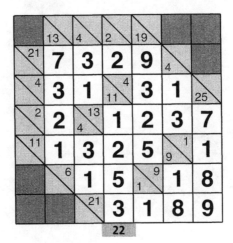

22

SOLUTIONS

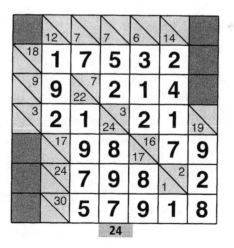

23

		10	1	10	4	12
	19\2	2	1	4	3	9
9	2	7	6\17	2	1	3
	6	1	2	3	6	
	3\6	12	8	1	3	1
7	1	2	4	3\8	2	1
18	2	4	3	8	1	

24

	12	7	7	6	14	
18	1	7	5	3	2	
9	9	7\22	2	1	4	
3	2	1	3\24	2	1	19
	17	9	8	16\17	7	9
	24	7	9	8	2\1	2
	30	5	7	9	1	8

SOLUTIONS

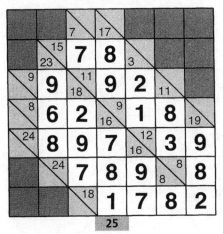

25

26

SOLUTIONS

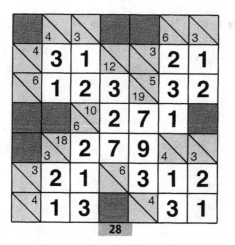

27

28

SOLUTIONS

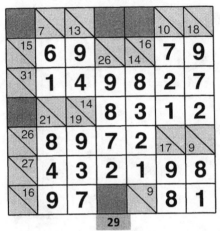

29

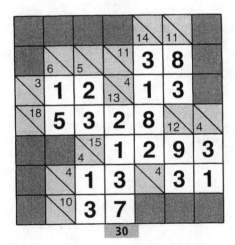

30

SOLUTIONS

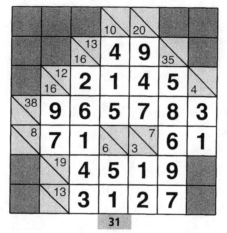

31

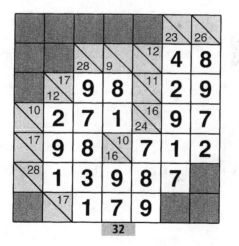

32

SOLUTIONS

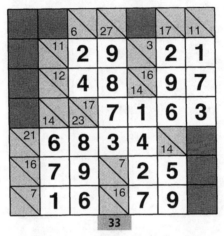

33

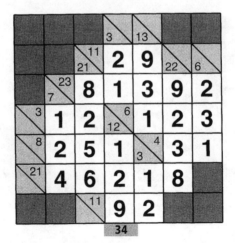

34

SOLUTIONS

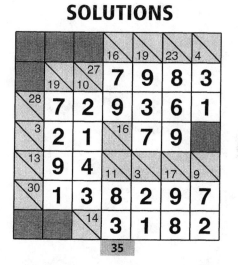

35

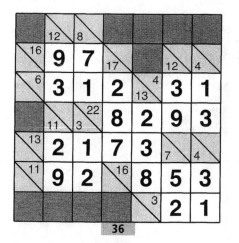

36

SOLUTIONS

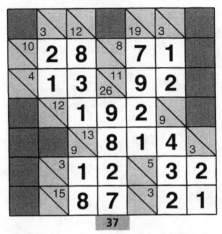

37

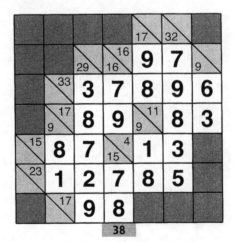

38

SOLUTIONS

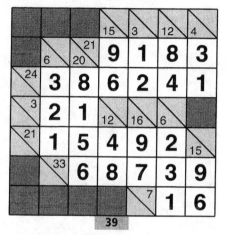

39

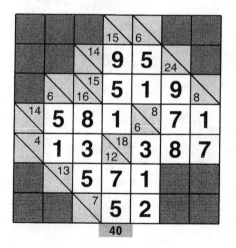

40

SOLUTIONS

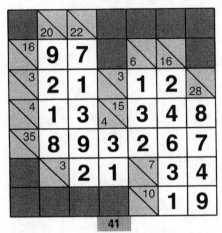

41

42

SOLUTIONS

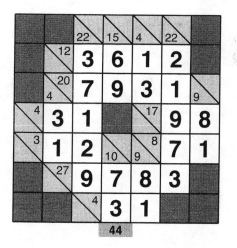

43

44

SOLUTIONS

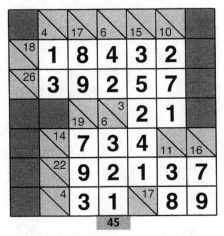

45

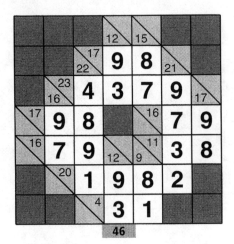

46

SOLUTIONS

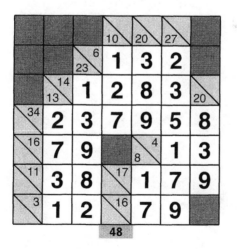

47

48

SOLUTIONS

Puzzle 49

Puzzle 50

SOLUTIONS

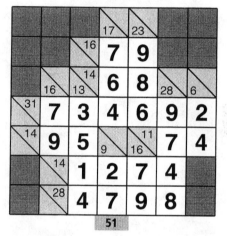

51

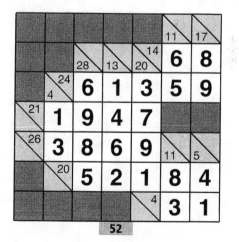

52

SOLUTIONS

53

	17	4	23		24	17
13	8	1	4	16	9	7
19	9	3	7	23 \ 8	7	1
	16	19 \ 27	3	7	8	9
29	7	8	9	5	17	16
17	8	9	20	3	8	9
3	1	2	24	8	9	7

54

	12	30			31	12
4	3	1		4	1	3
12	9	3	4	14 \ 12	3	9
	14	2	1	5	6	
	3 \ 27	8	3	9	7	14
8	1	7		13	5	8
11	2	9		15	9	6

SOLUTIONS

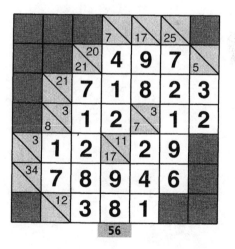

55

		4	11			9	12
11	**3**	**8**	13	22	4	**1**	**3**
30	**1**	**3**	**2**	**7**	**8**	**9**
		3	**1**	**2**		
	5	16 15	**7**	**9**	8	16
33	**2**	**8**	**3**	**4**	**7**	**9**
10	**3**	**7**		8	**1**	**7**

56

			7	17	25	
		20 21	**4**	**9**	**7**	5
	21	**7**	**1**	**8**	**2**	**3**
	3 8	**1**	**2**	7 3	**1**	**2**
3	**1**	**2**	11 17	**2**	**9**	
34	**7**	**8**	**9**	**4**	**6**	
	12	**3**	**8**	**1**		

SOLUTIONS

57

58

SOLUTIONS

Kakuro solution grids (puzzles 59 and 60).

59

		10	11		14	12		23	19
	3/8	1	2	5	4	1	17	8	9
12	1	2	9	16	7	9	4/8	1	3
10	7	3	6	18/19	1	2	3	5	7
	12	4	1	5	2	14	5	9	
		7	3	9	24			15	4
	14/4	1	2	3	8	11	12	9	3
3	1	2	10	2	7	1	3/6	2	1
7	3	4		21	9	5	3	4	
		13	5		13/3	2	1	26	
	3/6	2	1	12/12	1	3	2	6	9
16	1	6	4	2	3		17/4	9	8
4	3	1	16	9	7	11	3	7	1
6	2	4	3	1	2	5	1	4	

59

60

	14	12		22	25		5	11	
8	6	2	17	9	8	4	1	3	4
4	3	1	4	6	1	7	4	2	1
28	5	4	3	7	9	24	19/4	1	3
	6	5	1	29	7	8	9	5	
	4	19		7	3	1	2	21	
12	3	9	22/24	1	6	8	7	16	
3	1	2	21/7	8	4	9	14	5	9
	15	8	1	4	2		16	9	7
	13/25	4	9	11		17	26		
10/17	4	2	3	1	17/8	8	9	7	
16	9	7	9/22	3	1	9	7	2	
24	8	9	7	9	5	4	12	8	4
	7	5	2	5	2	3	3	2	1

60

SOLUTIONS

61

62

SOLUTIONS

63

```
     30  24      14  24      34  16
 17   9   8   8   1   7   16   9   7
 16
 4    7   9  10   2   8  17
                          24   8   9
 10
     1   2   7  27   8   9   7   3  24
                32
  4   3   1  17   1   3  23   8   6   9
                          38
     24   8   9   7  23   6   9   1   7
                       24
     32   3   8   9   7   5  15   7   8
     17  36  24   8   9   7   8   33
  9   8   1  23   2   8   3   1   9
                23
 29   9   7   8   5  24   9   7   8  16
                       29
     17   8   9  17   9   8  14   5   9
     24          19          20
 35   9   5   6   8   7  18   8   3   7
 16   7   9   7   2   5   4   3   1
 14   8   6  17   9   8  16   9   7
```

64

```
     19  25              26  14
 16   7   9   8          16   9   7
                          4
  7   2   4   1   9   7  16   1   4   2
 27   9   8   7   3  13   7   3   2   1
                    3
  4   1   3  17   6   2   9  12   8   4
                 4            4
      4   1   3  10   1  17   1   3
                    1     4
          4   1   3  11   8   3
                    9
             17   6   9   2   5
              3
             3   2   1  11   7   4  32
          20          13
      4   3   1   8   8  13   1   2  29
     22          3     13   3
  3   2   1  11   2   5   4  17   8   9
             17              17
 14   3   2   8   1  29   9   8   7   5
 23   8   6   9          23   9   6   8
 17   9   8              16   9   7
```

SOLUTIONS

65

66

SOLUTIONS

67

	2	16	11	8	9		5	5	29
32	2	9	7	8	6	9/6	5	3	1
10/21	7	3	9	8/9	3	5	8/6	2	6
3	3	16/4	1	3	6/7	1	5	8/3	8
8	1	7	11/10	6	5	10/6	1	2	7
17	7	9	1	3/12	2	1	4/13	1	3
4	4	13/7	9	4	12/11	5	7	4/10	4
8	6	2	17/14	8	9	7/10	6	1	35
13/27	5	8	12/5	2	3	15/8	9	6	
3	3	15/7	6	9	9/16	7	2	7/4	7
15	9	6	10/4	3	7	16/11	6	1	9
10	6	1	3	16/9	9	7	11/3	3	8
5	5	7/5	1	4	4/9	3	1	5/6	5
11	4	7	23	5	9	1	2	6	

68

			16	17		10	17		
		16/24	7	9	16	7	9	20	
	23/15	8	9	6	9/19	2	8	9	17
16	7	9	11/17	2	8	1	17/30	8	9
24	8	7	9	1/17	1	20/3	9	3	8
	16/17	17	8	9	9/24	2	7		
17	9	8	24/28	8	9	1	6	8	16
24	7	9	8	7/8	7	16/15	8	1	7
		29	9	5	8	7	16/11	7	9
	17	7/24	4	3	10/16	8	2	24/4	9
24	8	9	7	9/24	9	17	9	7	1
16	9	7	16/17	8	7	1	17/17	9	8
	24	8	9	7	24	7	9	8	
		17	8	9	17	9	8		

SOLUTIONS

Puzzle 69

			8	6		13	4		
		13/4	1	3	4	3	1	18	
	9/10	1	7	2	9/12	8	3	1	3
17	8	9	13/10	1	7	2	3/10	9	1
11	1	3	7	15/2	2	10/11	1	8	2
		8	1	7	13/9	7	2	7	8
3	4	14	2	8	1	3	12/12	5	7
6	2	1	3	13/9	9	3/9	6	2	1
4	1	3	4/12	6	3	2	1		
	12/10	10	3	7	9/4	1	3	14	8
12	9	2	1	18/1	1	19/18	2	9	7
4	3	1	4/11	1	8	2	9/4	3	1
	19	7	3	9	11	8	1	2	
		9	1	8	17	9	8		

69

Puzzle 70

		25	5		20	19		29	11
	11/3	1	2	16	9	7	17	9	8
13	2	8	3	4	1	3	9/16	8	1
16	9	7	24	26/13	3	9	7	5	2
	27	9	8	3	7	16	9	7	
	6/16	9	7	24			17	14	
17/18	1	7	2	8	20	13	8	5	
10	8	2	18	1	9	8	24/16	7	9
12	9	3		26	7	9	8	2	
		26	9		25/8	1	7	18	
17/17	9	8	10/26	8	2	9	7	16	
25	9	7	1	2	6		9/11	2	9
3	1	2	3	1	2	10	2	1	7
15	7	8	16	7	9	15	7	8	

70

SOLUTIONS

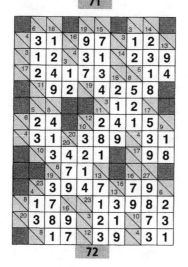

71

72

SOLUTIONS

73

74

SOLUTIONS

75

76

SOLUTIONS

77

	22	29					31	22
3	1	2	17			16 / 11	9	7
24	7	9	8	17		23 / 16	9	8	6
25	5	3	9	8	11	9	2	5	1
17	9	8	19 / 16	9	3	7	15 / 5	7	8
	16	7	9	8 / 24	8	5 / 18	3	2
		15	7	8	10	8	2
		24 / 8	7	8	9	16
	10 / 24	1	9	8 / 17	1	7	27
15 / 19	8	7	12 / 8	8	16 / 9	9	7	26
17	8	9	13 / 17	3	9	1	16 / 16	9	7
28	7	4	8	9	18	8	7	1	2
13	3	1	9			19	9	2	8
3	1	2				17	8	9

78

			8	12				
		16	7	9	20		
	14	8	12	1	2	9	18
6	5	1	6	16	1	8	7	13
18	9	7	2	13	6	3	2	1	18
	12	22 / 12	3	9	10	20	9	3	8
21	6	9	1	3	2	9	12 / 3	2	1
10	3	7	30	1	5	6	2	7	9
3	2	1	20	6	3	2	1	6	22
12	1	3	8	12	11	1	3	2	5
	6	2	3	1	10	15	6	1	8
	12	9	2	1	4	12	3	9
	19	9	7	3			
	3	2	1			

SOLUTIONS

79

	27	13	2		3	1	17	4	8
9	1	6	2	20/11	2	1	6	3	8
12	5	7	7/5	6	1	5/3	4	1	24
3	3	9/13	4	5	9/10	2	7	3/14	3
13	7	5	1	3/11	2	1	6/5	5	1
17	9	8	15/15	7	8	18/11	1	9	8
2	2	11/16	7	4	13/14	9	4	15/7	7
26/15	7	8	8/10	6	2	14/14	9	5
10	1	9	11/11	3	8	14/6	8	6	28
7	7	10/9	3	7	8/6	2	6	9/17	9
23	9	6	8	9/17	5	4	10/8	9	1
8	5	3	5/16	4	1	17/9	6	8	3
4	4	15/8	7	8	9/4	7	2	7/5	7
28	8	9	5	4	2	13	5	8

80

	11	27		21	16		13	3	
4	3	1	10	3	7	4	3	1	
11	8	3	17/4	8	9	11/10	9	2	
16/11	8	1	7	4/18	3	1	6	11
23	2	4	3	1	6	7	3/14	1	2
3	1	2	11/15	2	9	14/16	2	3	9
19	8	9	2	16/5	3	7	4	2
4/12	1	3	16/16	9	7	30	7
13/3	1	3	2	7	11/23	1	8	2
19	2	8	9	4/5	1	3	8/4	7	1
4	1	3	27/12	2	8	1	3	9	4
10/5	2	3	6/4	2	1	3	4
17	8	9	12	3	9	3	2	1
3	2	1	9	1	8	4	1	3

SOLUTIONS

81

Grid clues and answers:

			4	15	9		
		19 / 22	3	9	7	16	
	16 / 10	3	1	6	2	4	21
3	2	1			15	6	9
16	7	9			11	3	8
6	1	5	17	6	4 / 5	1	4
	21	4	9	5	1	2	
		12	8	1	3		

82

	6	26		24	18	11	4
4	1	3	14	7	2	4	1
13	5	8	20 / 35	9	1	7	3
	28	6	9	8	5	18	
	17	9	8	16 / 21	7	9	
	4 / 17	20	7	9	3	1	6
26	3	9	6	8	9	5	4
18	1	8	5	4	5	3	2

SOLUTIONS

83

84

SOLUTIONS

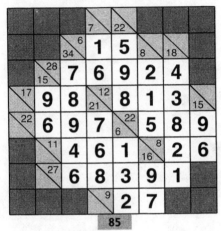

85

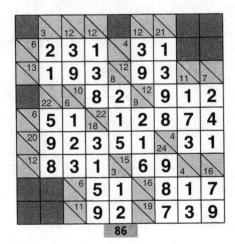

86

SOLUTIONS

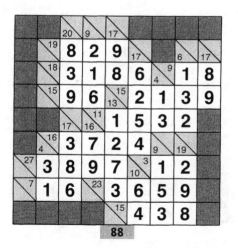

87

88

SOLUTIONS

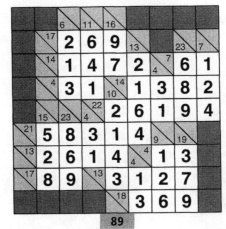

89

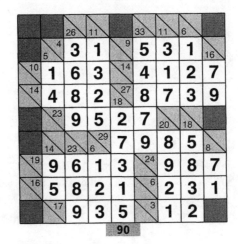

90

SOLUTIONS

91

Grid 91 (Kakuro solution):

			4\	14\		10\	12\		
		\5 22\	1	4	\10	2	8	\26	
	\12 4\	1	3	8	\7 12\	1	4	2	\6
\12	3	9	\9 26\	2	3	4	\14 28\	9	5
\18	1	8	9	\25 15\	9	3	4	8	1
	\13	4	3	6		\16 16\	9	7	
	\17 22\	8	9	\14	9	5	\18		
\3 5\	2	1	\23	\18 4\	7	8	3	\16	
\21	4	9	5	2	1	\10 15\	2	1	7
\4	1	3	\20 4\	8	3	9	\15 12\	6	9
	\13	8	1	4	\22	5	9	8	
		\12	3	9	\4	1	3		

92

Grid 92 (Kakuro solution):

		15\	3\				12\	12\	
	\5 4\	4	1	\10	\4		\11 16\	2	9
\22	3	9	2	7	1	\6 16\	2	1	3
\3	1	2	\21 5\	2	3	6	1	9	
	\4 11\	3	1	\17	8	9	\11 16\		
\9 10\	7	2		\14	2	4	1	7	
\11	8	3	\10	\15		\16 9\	7	9	
\11	2	1	3	5	\5 13\	2	3		
	\3 6\	2	1	\16 17\	9	7	\24 10\		
\23 17\	2	1	9	8	3	\13 9\	9	4	
\14	9	1	4	\26	9	1	3	7	6
\11	8	3			\14	6	8		

SOLUTIONS

Puzzle 93

			11	4	27		
13	6	6	**2**	**1**	**3**		12	3
14 **9**	**5**	11 18 **1**	**3**	**7**	8 10 **7**	**1**
18 **4**	**1**	**8**	**5**	16 **8**	**1**	**5**	**2**
19	9 10 **7**	**3**	13 **9**	**4**	22 11
18 **9**	**6**	**3**			22 **5**	**9**	**8**
3 **2**	**1**	20			6 17 **5**	**1**
15 **8**	**2**	**5**	26	11 19 **1**	**8**	**2**
13 4 16 **9**	**7**	17 **8**	**9**	10 15
26 **8**	**3**	**6**	**9**	22 3 **3**	**7**	**4**	**8**
6 **5**	**1**	14 **6**	**1**	**7**	13 **6**	**7**
		7 **4**	**2**	**1**		

Puzzle 94

		17	10			
17 20 **8**	**9**	9	19	11
25 16 **8**	**9**	**1**	**7**	17 16 **9**	**8**	17
10 **9**	**1**	11	21 **2**	**4**	**6**	**1**	**8**
10 **7**	**2**	**1**	16 24 **1**	**4**	**2**	**9**
17 **9**	**8**	17 20 **9**	**8**	16
24 **2**	**4**	**8**	**3**	**7**	26
5 19 13 8 **1**	**7**	17 **8**	**9**	16
28 **4**	**9**	**7**	**8**	16 **1**	**8**	**7**
30 **1**	**8**	**5**	**7**	**9**	5 16 16 **7**	**9**
3 **2**	**1**	21 **7**	**3**	**9**	**2**
		9 **2**	**7**	

SOLUTIONS

95

				8	19			22	5
	11	8	4	1	3		8/23	7	1
4	3	1	13/10	5	8	21	8	9	4
25	8	5	9	2	1	15/21	9	6	
	3	2	1	6/29	2	3	1	4	8
8	16	32/19	7	5	9	2	3	6	
23	6	7	2	8	11/27	5	3	1	2
24	2	9	1	5	3	4	12	24	
	20/7	3	9	8	17/11	9	8	9	
11/15	2	9	26	5	1	3	9	8	
12	7	1	4	16	9	7	8	7	1
12	8	4		5	2	3			

96

	9	30		15	19		10	6	4
16	7	9	14	6	8	6	1	2	3
5	2	3	3/4	1	3	11/16	6	4	1
30/14	2	1	8	7	9	3	6	23	
18	9	7	2	8	1	7	11/25	2	9
4	3	1	20		21	20/4	9	3	8
17	2	8	7	24/16	9	3	5	1	6
20	6/28	6	9	8	1	4	22	6	
17	3	1	2	7	4	10	7	1	2
15	8	2	5	6	15	5/3	4	1	
12	9	3	14/4	1	3	9/11	1	5	3
12/4	30	4	5	9	7	2	3	3	
20	9	3	8	3	2	1	9	7	2
6	3	1	2	4	1	3	3	2	1

SOLUTIONS

97

98

SOLUTIONS

				23\	14\	10\			
			19\23	8	9	6	22\		
		13\23	4	6	5	1	7	15\	
	23\20	6	5	9	\14	3	9	2	10\
\11	8	1	2	17\		25\7	4	1	2
\26	9	4	8	5	20\11	5	2	3	1
\8	6	2	\23	6	9	8	\16	9	7
	19\	11\	\15	3	8	4		14\	24\
\3	2	1	21\6	2	3	1	10\8	1	7
\14	8	2	3	1	\20	7	3	2	8
\18	9	3	6	19\		7\21	4	8	9
	\21	5	7	9	12\6	2	1	3	
		\28	5	8	9	4	2		
			\6	2	3	1			

99

	11\	24\	4\			20\	3\		
\10	3	6	1		20\11	9	2		
\17	5	9	3	10\11	7	3	1	20\	3\
\3	1	2	13\24	7	9	8	9\4	3	1
\17	2	7	3	1	4	14\17	6	9	2
	12\	8\11	9	2	6\12	3	1	8	
\13	7	5	1	23\10	3	5	2	10\	21\
\3	2	1	24\16	8	2	6	30\5	1	4
\19	3	2	7	6	1	11\14	4	2	8
	11\	29\17	8	9	11\28	8	7	4	9
\19	3	7	9	19\11	1	2	5	3	
\16	7	9	17\16	9	4	1	2	6\	4\
\23	1	5	8	3	6	\16	9	4	3
	\24	8	9	7		\6	3	2	1

100

SOLUTIONS

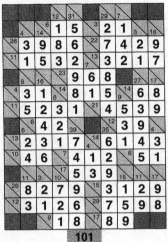

101

Printed in the United States
By Bookmasters